How to Write a

Book Report,

Book Review,

or Literary Analysis

Step-by-Step Study Skills

www.HappyFrogLearning.com

Table of Contents

Introduction

Welcome to the **How to Write a Book Report, Book Review, or Literary Analysis** workbook.

Book assignments in middle and high school can vary from a short summary of the plot, to writing about something called a 'literary device'. As a student, you might be confused about what the teacher expects.

Don't worry, this workbook will support you, whether you are writing a:

- Book report
- Book review
- Novel study
- Literary criticism
- Any other assignment related to a fiction or non-fiction book, movie, poem or play.

Because there are so many different terms, we're going to use the generic term 'book report' throughout this book. We'll also assume you are writing about a book or movie. However, the strategies we introduce are appropriate for ANY of the types of assignments mentioned above.

The first section of the book is the workbook part. Follow this from beginning to end to learn a step-by-step procedure for how to complete a book report.

In the second half of the book, you can find a reference section that explains many common literary devices that teachers might mention. There's also a FAQ that covers the minor differences you need to consider in case you are:

- Doing a review or a literary analysis instead of a book report
- Analysing a movie, play or poem instead of a book
- Or reading non-fiction instead of fiction

Let's get started.

A Note about Examples

This book is designed for students from middle school through high school and early college. So our examples reflect that. Some are easier, some are harder.

We put the easier examples first. But the last example or practice question may contain topics you are not familiar with. Don't worry! Just skip it.

Part 1

Writing a Book Report

Writing a book report consists of four stages.

1. **Before You Read**

   In this stage you review your assignment instructions to understand the type of information you will look for as you read the book. You prepare your reading questions to match the requirements.

2. **While You Read**

   In this stage you read the book, completing the reading questions as you go.

3. **After You Read**

   During this stage you use your notes to create your thesis statement and outline.

4. **Writing the Report**

   Now you are ready to write your report, using the paragraph-by-paragraph guide.

In this workbook, you will learn how to do each of these steps.

Step 1

Before You Read

Did you know... reading the book is NOT the first task when doing a book report!

When you read a book for a book report, you are not just reading to enjoy the book. You are also reading to **gather information** for your review or report.

The purpose of the *Before You Read* activities is to make sure you know what information you need to gather as you read the book.

There are five tasks that need to be completed in this step. We will learn about these one-by-one.

1.1   Analyze the Assignment Instructions

1.2   Review Unknown Words

1.3   Choose Your Book

1.4   Understand the Genre Expectations

1.5   Prepare Reading Questions

1.1 Analyze the Assignment Instructions

LEARN

When you read a book for a school book report, you must **gather information** as you read. You will use this information to support your opinions in your report.

How do you know what information to gather? You review the instructions from the teacher. The instructions will tell you what your teacher expects to see in your assignment.

Let's look at some examples. Below are three essay topics. For each, we have noted what information we should track so that we can answer the book report question.

Book Report Topic	Information to Track when Reading
How does Laura's character change in the book *By the Shores of Silver Lake* by Laura Ingalls Wilder?	How does Laura behave at the beginning compared to how she behaves at the end of the book? What different choices does she make? What causes her to make the different choices?
Choose a book set in an unusual location. How does the setting influence the story?	How is the setting unusual? When does the setting influence the story? What would be different in an alternate setting?
How does ambition influence the characters in Shakespeare's *Macbeth*?	Which characters show ambition? What choices do these characters make that are influenced by ambition?

1.1 Analyze the Assignment Instructions

PRACTICE

Now it's your turn. For each essay topic in the table below, note down the type of information you need to look for while you read the book.

Essay Topic	Information to Track when Reading
In the novel *Hatchet*, what important lessons does Brian learn about nature during his time in the wilderness?	
Discuss the theme in the novel *Hatchet*. (Theme = the message the reader can take away from the book)	
In the novel *Call of the Wild*, how does the author make Buck the dog seem like a human?	
Describe the conflict in the book you chose. (Conflict = the problems the character faces)	
Discuss the use of allegory in George Orwell's *Animal Farm*. (Don't know what an allegory is? Skip this one!)	

1.2 Review Unknown Words

LEARN

"Review Unknown Words" – sounds a bit scary, huh? Don't worry, this just means you should **understand all the words** that the teacher uses in the assignment.

Your book assignment may use words such as 'theme', 'point of view', 'figurative language', etc. Before you read your book, make sure you understand any unfamiliar words. You can use the reference section in Part 2 of this book if you need help.

Below is an example that uses some unfamiliar words. We wrote down our own definition of the word to make sure we understood it.

Assignment: Discuss the use of **allegory** in George Orwell's *Animal Farm* and how the allegory is shown through **imagery**.

Literary Term	My definition
Allegory	An allegory is a story in which a character, setting or event is used to deliver a message about real world issues and events. For example, in *The Sneetches* by Dr Seuss, the real message is about racism.
Imagery	**Imagery** is writing that uses all the human senses, such as sight, hearing, taste, touch, and smell, when telling the story. Writers often use **figurative language** to create imagery.
Figurative language	Figurative language is when words have an extra meaning beyond the literal or 'regular' meaning of the words. Idioms are an example of figurative language.

1.2 Review Unknown Words

PRACTICE

Now it's time to practice. For each assignment, look up any words that you don't know in the reference section at the back of the book. Write a definition in your own words.

And don't worry if you've never heard of these words. That's why I chose them!

Assignment 1: Describe the **conflict** in the book you chose.

Assignment 2: Discuss how the **theme** of your book relates to the modern world.

Assignment 3: In the novel *Call of the Wild*, to what extent does the author **anthropomorphize** Buck?

Literary Term	My Definition

1.3 Choose Your Book

LEARN

Sometimes the teacher will assign a book. Other times you will be allowed to choose your own book. Your choice of book can make your book report harder to do, or easier. Use the following guidelines to make your task easier!

If you are allowed to choose your own book, consider the following:

- Choose a book of a **suitable reading level**. Don't choose one that is too easy or too hard.

- Choose a book that is **interesting to you**.

- Choose a book that your **teacher approves** of.

  Make sure to check with your teacher that your choice of book is okay. If you can explain the reasons for your choice, your teacher is likely to approve... assuming your reasons make sense!

- Choose a book that **suits the type of assignment** you have.

  If your assignment has questions about the characters, choose a book that has interesting characters. A librarian can help you choose a suitable book if you explain your assignment to them.

1.4 Understand the Genre Expectations

LEARN

Books can be categorized according to **genre.** The genre identifies the type of story the book contains. Examples of genres are science fiction, thriller, etc.

Each genre has specific **reader expectations**. That means that readers expect to find specific types of things in different genres.

For example, a murder mystery typically has a murder, several suspects and a detective who solves the crime. It's not really a murder mystery if those things aren't in the book.

Make sure you know the genre of your book. Also make sure you know what readers expect from this genre. You should be able to explain the expectations in your own words. If you're not sure, an internet search will help.

As you read, you can compare your book to what is expected.

Here's an example of my explanation of the science fiction genre.

Genre	My Explanation of Reader Expectations
Science Fiction	• Set in the future or in a faraway world. • Contains technologies that don't exist yet. • May include space travel or time travel.

1.4 Understand the Genre Expectations

PRACTICE

Now it's your turn. Look up some information about each of these genres. Explain them using your own words.

Choose your own genre for the last line.

Genre	My Explanation of Reader Expectations
Fantasy	
Cozy Mystery	
Young Adult/ Coming of Age	

1.5 Prepare Reading Questions

LEARN

Your final task before reading the book is to prepare your 'reading questions.' These are the questions you will ask yourself as you read the book.

You figure out your questions by considering:

- Your analysis of the assignment.

- Your knowledge of the book genre.

For example, let's imagine your assignment is about **conflict** in a **spy** novel. ('Conflict' refers to the problems that the main character faces in the book.) In this case, your reading questions could be:

1. What problems did the main character face in this chapter?

2. What did the main character do in this chapter to try and resolve the problems?

3. Who/what is causing a problem for the main character? Is the conflict 'character vs character', 'character vs nature', or something different?

4. Does the conflict meet the expectations for a spy novel?

5. Is the conflict unusual or interesting, or is it predictable?

As you read your book, you will gather information to answer these questions. You can either note the information as you come across it, or review the questions after each scene or chapter.

1.5 Prepare Reading Questions

PRACTICE

Now it's your turn to practice. Write 3-5 reading questions for each assignment below. You can refer back to the assignment analysis shown earlier in the book.

Assignment: How does Laura's character change in the book *By the Shores of Silver Lake* by Laura Ingalls Wilder?

My Questions:

Assignment: In the novel *Call of the Wild*, how does the author make Buck the dog seem like a human?

My Questions:

Step 2

While You Read

You are now ready to read the book! There are two tasks that need to be completed in this stage.

    2.1   Plan Your Reading Schedule

    2.2   Read & Take Notes

2.1 Plan Your Reading Schedule

LEARN

You have two main tasks to do between now and when the book report is due. These are to **read** the book and **write** the report.

It is important to allow enough time for each of these tasks.

As a rough guide, divide the time between now and the assignment due date into two. The first half of the time is for reading the book. The remaining time is for writing and editing the book report.

Next, calculate how many pages you need to read each day to finish the book in time. To do this, divide the number of pages by the number of days you have to read the book.

$$\frac{\text{NUMBER OF PAGES}}{\text{NUMBER OF DAYS}} = \text{PAGES PER DAY}$$

For example, if you have 20 days to read a 200-page book, then you should read about 10 pages per day.

PRACTICE

Calculate how many pages per day you should read if you have to read a 150-page book in 10 days.

$$\frac{\qquad}{} = $$

2.2 Read & Take Notes

LEARN

You now get to read the book! Yay!

As you read, it is important that you watch out for sections that will be helpful in your book report. If you find something useful, NOTE IT DOWN.

NOTE IT DOWN is in capitals because it is very important that you write down the information. You might think you will remember, but chances are you won't remember... or you will remember, but you will spend a lot of time trying to find the information again. So, make notes as you go.

You can make notes by:

- Using post-it notes inserted into the book,

- Writing in a notebook,

- Taking photos and adding notes to them.

Use whatever technique works for you. But make sure you take relevant notes as you read the book.

So how do you know what to take notes on?

Use the Reading Questions you created in Step 1 as the basis for what to take notes on.

For example, if your assignment is about how a character changes during the book, and your reading questions are:

1. What decisions does Laura make in this chapter?

2. What influences her decision?

2.2 Read & Take Notes

LEARN continued

Then, some notes you might make are:

- Laura is middle sister, but has to start acting like the oldest sister because of Mary's blindness. E.g. She acts as Mary's eyes by describing things.
- Laura changes her goal to become a school teacher to help the family pay for Mary's expenses.

At a minimum, you should answer your Reading Questions at the end of each chapter. Ideally, you will do this AND make a note whenever you come across something that might be useful.

What information should I include in my notes?

When you do make a note, make sure to include:

- What is interesting/useful,
- What page it is on, and
- Why it is interesting/useful.

Step 3

After You Read

You have finished reading the book and taking notes. You are now ready to begin planning your book report. In this section, we cover the following topics.

3.1   What is a Thesis Statement?

3.2   Making a Claim

3.3   Finding Reasons to Support Your Claim

3.4   Combining Claim and Reasons to Make a Thesis Statement.

3.5   Convert the Thesis Statement into an Outline

3.1 What is a Thesis Statement?

LEARN

The first step in preparing to write your book report is to create a **thesis statement**. That sounds difficult, but a thesis statement is just **a claim (statement of what you think)** and three **supporting reasons (why you think it).**

THESIS = CLAIM + 3 REASONS

For example, here is a thesis statement for an assignment about the novel *Hatchet*:

Through the challenges of finding food, building a shelter and trying to stay calm, Brian changes from a child into a young man.

Claim: Brian changes from a child into a young man.

3 Reasons/evidence are:

- His experiences in finding food,

- His experiences in building a shelter,

- And his experiences with trying to stay calm.

After reading a thesis statement, the reader will have a clear understanding of:

- The point (or argument) you will make in the essay. (What you think.)

- The type of evidence/examples you will use to support that claim. (Why you think it.)

From this thesis statement we can tell:

- The writer will show how Brian has matured from a child to a young adult.

- The writer will use examples from how Brian survived in the wilderness.

24

3.1 What is a Thesis Statement?

LEARN Continued

Sometimes an author might use a simpler thesis statement that summarizes the reasons, instead of listing each individual reason. For example, here is a shorter thesis statement about *Animal Farm*:

> *In Animal Farm, the actions of the pigs demonstrate that more power leads to more corruption.*

From this thesis statement, we can tell that the writer will use evidence about the pigs' actions to prove her claim. As yet, we don't know what three reasons the author will use to support her claim. But, we do know that all reasons will be about the pigs' actions.

WHY IS A THESIS STATEMENT IMPORTANT?

Having a strong thesis statement is **the most important** part of your book report. The thesis statement is important because it summarizes your entire book report in one sentence.

From that one sentence, your teacher will know how well you understand the assignment. She will also have a good idea about the quality of your report. Make sure you spend enough time to ensure you have a **strong thesis statement.**

Having a strong thesis statement also makes the writing of your report much easier. You'll see how in the next sections.

Now, let's learn **how** to create a strong thesis statement. First, we'll focus on how to make a claim. Then we'll focus on finding the three supporting reasons.

3.2 Craft a Claim for Your Thesis Statement

LEARN

The first step in creating a thesis statement is to **make a claim.** That is, you should state something that you believe to be true.

Your claim should be **provable** and should **directly answer your book assignment**.

> **Provable** means that you can provide evidence or reasons that support the truth of your claim.
>
> **Directly related to the assignment** means that your claim should answer the question in the assignment.

For example, if your book assignment asks about the theme, your claim should be about the theme.

If your book assignment asks about character development, your claim should be about a character's development.

Let's look at some examples of both good and bad claims.

Assignment:

> In the novel *Hatchet*, what important lessons does Brian learn about nature?

Strong Claims:

> Brian learns that nature needs to be respected, but that nature also provides.
>
> Brian learns to work with nature in order to survive.

Each of the two strong claims can be proven or disproven. And both claims relate directly to the assignment topic.

3.2 Craft a Claim for Your Thesis Statement

LEARN Continued

Mismatched Claim:

> Brian learns he can rely on himself.

The mismatched claim can be proven or disproven. However, it does not directly relate to the assignment topic. The assignment topic asks about what Brian learns about **nature**.

How do you come up with a claim?

The simplest way to come up with a claim is to:

- Review the notes you made while you read the book, and

- Think about what sort of claim those notes could support.

Try out different ideas until you find one you think is strong.

For each possible claim, make sure you evaluate whether it is **provable** using evidence from the book and whether it is **directly related to the assignment**.

As a next step, you'll practice making some claims. After that, you'll learn how to find supporting reasons for your claim.

3.2 Craft a Claim for Your Thesis Statement

PRACTICE

Now it's your turn to practice. It is pretty much impossible to come up with a claim if you haven't read the book. So, in the following exercises you will use books or movies that you have already seen/read.

Come up with a claim (or two) for each of these assignments.

Assignment	Your Claim(s)
Discuss the theme of *your favorite movie/book.* (Theme = message you can take away from the book.)	
How are the main character and the bad guy similar in *your favorite movie/book.*	
Give your opinion on the main character's actions in *your favorite movie/book.*	
Discuss how the setting influenced the story of *your favorite movie/book.*	

3.3 Identify the Supporting Reasons

LEARN

Now that you have your claim, the next step is to come up with some supporting reasons.

Start with the question: **Why do I think the claim is true?**

Note down as many reasons as you can think of why your claim is true. Next, refer to your reading notes and see if you can find more reasons and examples of why your claim is true.

After you have gathered all possible reasons, review your list and choose the three which you think are the strongest. Strong reasons have these characteristics:

1. Your reasons provide **strong support** for your claim.

2. You **have examples** from the text for each of the reasons.

3. Your reasons **do not overlap**. (You're not saying the same thing twice.)

4. You have **not found any strong arguments for the opposite view.**

Let's take a look at an example. Let's imagine our claim about Brian from *Hatchet* is:

Brian changes from a child into a mature young man.

Here are some reasons to support the claim that Brian becomes more mature.

1. Brian learns patience.

   - E.g. At the beginning of the novel, Brian has big reactions when things go badly. Towards the end he has more patience and can handle when bad things happen.

3.3 Identify the Supporting Reasons

LEARN continued

2. Brian learns new skills.

- E.g. At first Brian cannot find the birds he is hunting. However, after he trains his eyes to spot their outline, he successfully hunts them. .

3. Brian develops independence

- At the beginning Brian waits to be rescued. As the book progresses, Brian takes responsibility for himself. At the end, he even offers the arriving bush-pilot some food.

Each of these reasons and examples show how Brian is maturing. They support the claim that Brian matures from a child to a young man.

You will see I have already started noting down the examples which support each reason. That will come in handy when it's time to make an outline.

Also, the three reasons are separate topics, they do not say the same thing in two different ways.

Final Note: We introduced the steps of 'making a claim' and 'finding reasons' as two separate steps in order to explain each of them clearly.

However, when you are doing a real assignment, you will find that you do both together. You will consider reasons and try out claims and then repeat that process several times until you have a strong claim and supporting reasons.

3.3 Identify the Supporting Reasons

PRACTICE

Practice Time!

Review one of the claims you made in the last exercise and come up with 3-5 supporting reasons. Identify which reasons you think are the strongest.

Book/Movie:	
Your Claim:	
Supporting Reasons:	

3.4 Combine Claim and Reasons to Make Thesis Statement

LEARN

You have done the hard work. In this section you combine your claim and reasons into a thesis statement... and it won't take you long at all!

The simplest way to create a thesis statement is to use a template like this one:

CLAIM because REASON 1, REASON 2, and REASON 3.

For example:

Brian changes from a child into a mature young man through the challenges of finding food, building a shelter and trying to stay positive.

Alternatively:

Because of REASON 1, REASON 2 and REASON 3, CLAIM.

Through the challenges of finding food, building a shelter and trying to stay positive, Brian changes from a child into a mature young man.

Sometimes, it is better to use a shorter version of the thesis statement. In a shorter version, you summarize (combine) the reasons instead of listing them one by one.

Through the challenges of surviving in the wilderness, Brian changes from a child into a mature young man.

And now you have your thesis statement!

3.4 Combine Claim and Reasons to Make Thesis Statement

PRACTICE

Now it's your turn to practice. Choose a book or movie you are familiar with. Create a claim and then come up with 3-5 reasons that support your claim. Next, combine the claim and reasons into a thesis statement.

Your Book/Movie	
Claim	
Supporting Reason 1	
Supporting Reason 2	
Supporting Reason 3	
Thesis Statement	

3.5 Convert Thesis Statement to Outline

LEARN

The final step before writing is to convert your thesis statement into an outline.

An **outline** shows the structure of your report. It shows you what to write about in each paragraph.

Because you already have a thesis statement, creating the outline is easy.

Take the notes you have created so far and write them out like this:

Introduction:

Thesis statement

Body Paragraph 1:

Reason 1 + Examples

Body Paragraph 2:

Reason 2 + Examples

Body Paragraph 3:

Reason 3 + Examples

Conclusion:

Reworded Thesis Statement

That's your outline!

Let's see how we do this with our example from *Hatchet*.

3.5 Convert Thesis Statement to Outline

LEARN continued

Introduction:

Thesis statement: By learning patience, building new skills and developing self-reliance, Brian shows that he has matured from a child into a young man.

Body Paragraph 1:

Reason 1: Brian learns patience.

Examples: At the beginning of the novel, Brian has big reactions when things go badly. Towards the end he has more patience and can handle when bad things happen.

Body Paragraph 2:

Reason 2: Brian learns new skills.

Examples: At first Brian cannot locate the birds he is hunting. After he trains his eyes to spot their outline, however, he successfully hunts them.

Body Paragraph 3:

Reason 3: Brian develops self-reliance.

Examples: At the beginning Brian waits to be rescued. As the book progresses, Brian takes responsibility for himself, and at the end even offers the arriving bush-pilot some food.

Conclusion:

Reworded Thesis: Through the challenge of surviving in the wilderness, Brian matures from a child into a young man.

I now have my outline and I am ready to write!

3.5 Convert Thesis Statement to Outline

PRACTICE

Now it's your turn to practice. Use any of the books/movies you have used in previous exercises and convert your notes into an outline.

Thesis Statement	
Reason 1 + Examples	
Reason 2 + Examples	
Reason 3 + Examples	
Conclusion	

Step 4

Writing the Report

Now that you have your book report outline, the next step is to write the book report. A book report has three types of paragraphs:

1. Introductory or First Paragraph

2. Body Paragraphs

3. Conclusion or Final Paragraph

In this section, you will learn how to write each of these types of paragraphs.

4.1 Writing the Introductory Paragraph

LEARN

The introductory paragraph is the first paragraph in your report. The introductory paragraph consists of three parts:

- The hook

- A short introduction to the book

- The thesis statement

In this section, you will learn how to write each of these parts. (Except for the thesis statement, which you have already written!)

Here's an example, broken up so you can see each section.

Introductory Paragraph Parts	Example
Hook	What would you do if you had to survive in the wilderness?
Book Summary	*Hatchet*, by Gary Paulsen, tells the story of 13-year-old Brian, who is forced to survive alone in after his plane crashes in the wilderness.
Thesis Statement	In this book, the challenge of surviving alone forces Brian to mature from a child into a young man.

4.1 Introduction: Writing the Hook

LEARN

The hook is the very first sentence of your essay. The purpose of the hook is to grab your reader's attention.

Here are some suggestions for creating an interesting hook.

- **Ask a question** that's relevant to your thesis statement. Make sure it's not a question that everyone knows the answer to. The question should make the reader start to think.

- **Include an interesting fact**. This fact could be about the setting or plot of the book.

- **Include a relevant quotation** from someone famous or from a character in the book. The quotation must relate to your thesis statement.

- **Begin with a compelling or unexpected statement**. Again, it must be related to your claim or thesis statement.

There is no single 'correct' hook. So, brainstorm/research a few and choose the one you prefer best.

See the next page for an example of each of these types of hooks.

4.1 Introduction: Writing the Hook

LEARN continued

Here are some sample hooks for a report about *Hatchet*.

Thesis Statement	Brian's wilderness experience turns him from a child into a young man
Potential Hooks	Could you survive alone in the wilderness?
	According to a study by the Transportation Safety Board of Canada, only about 10% of occupants escape from float planes that crash in water. Brian Robeson, in Gary Paulsen's novel *Hatchet*, was extremely lucky.
	Forty-two days had passed since he had died and been born as the new Brian. (*Hatchet*, Chapter 13)
	It took only 54 days to change Brian from a child into a young man.

As a contrast, these hooks don't quite work for this thesis statement.

- He was alone. In a roaring plane with no pilot he was alone. Alone. *Hatchet*, Chapter 1.

  This is a dramatic hook, but it does not really relate to the claim of new-found maturity or wilderness survival. It would be a good hook for a different claim.

- Did you know it is difficult to light a fire without matches or a lighter?

  The problem with this hook is that it asks a question that everyone knows the answer to. It does not make a good hook.

4.1 Introduction: Writing the Hook

PRACTICE

Research/brainstorm 3 hooks for two books/movies of your choice. You can use thesis statements from previous practice pages.

Book/Movie + Thesis Statement	
Potential Hooks	

Book/Movie + Thesis Statement	
Potential Hooks	

4.1 Introduction: Introducing the Book

LEARN

In the first paragraph, you tell your readers some basic details about your book. The details should include **the title, the author, and a short book summary**.

For fiction, your summary should introduce the main character and the plot. You can use this template to make it easier.

WHO, DID WHAT, WHERE/WHEN & WHY

For example:

> *Hatchet*, by Gary Paulsen, tells the story of 13-year-old Brian, who has to survive alone in the wild after his plane crashes.

This statement tells us:

> WHO: 13-year-old Brian
>
> DID WHAT: survived alone
>
> WHERE/WHEN: in the wild, occurs in modern times because a plane is mentioned
>
> WHY: because of a plane crash
>
> The sentence also includes the title and author.

In this example, all the information was included in one sentence. However, it's okay if you need more than one sentence.

4.1 Introduction: Introducing the Book

LEARN

For non-fiction, your book summary should state the type of information the book includes and who it is written for.

You should also include the title and author or publisher. The following templates can help.

TITLE, ABOUT WHAT, FOR WHO

TITLE, FOR WHO, ABOUT WHAT

For example:

A Child Through Time, by DK Publishers, shows the children of today how children lived in the past.

In this example we see:

FOR WHO (the children of today) and

ABOUT WHAT (how children lived in the past).

The sentence also includes the title and publisher.

How do I know which to include? The author or the publisher?

Not sure which to include? Look at the cover of the book. If the author's name is there, use that. If it is not, use the publisher name.

4.1 Introduction: Introducing the Book

PRACTICE

Now it's your turn to create a brief book introduction. Choose two fiction and two non-fiction books and write a short book summary for each.

Book	Brief Summary

4.1 Complete Introduction Paragraph

PRACTICE

You are now ready to write a complete introductory paragraph. You can write a paragraph about a fiction or non-fiction book or video.

You can use any of the examples you have created in previous practices.

Don't forget to include a hook, a book summary and your thesis statement.

_____

_____

_____

_____

_____

_____

_____

4.2 Writing the Body Paragraphs

LEARN

Body paragraphs are the main part of the book report. They come after the introduction paragraph. Each body paragraph provides evidence that supports your claim.

A body paragraph consists of three parts.

- A topic sentence

- Supporting examples and quotes

- A link back to claim/thesis statement

Here's an example of a body paragraph for a fiction book report. The topic sentence and link back to the claim have been highlighted in grey.

Thesis statement:

In the novel *Hatchet*, the challenge of surviving alone forces Brian to mature from a child into a young man.

Sample body paragraph:

One sign of increasing maturity is that Brian stops blaming other people for things going wrong. For example, early in the book, Brian thinks that if his mother hadn't forced the divorce, Brian wouldn't be stuck in the wilderness. Later on in chapter 15, even when a tornado happens, Brian doesn't worry about blaming anyone and instead just gets on with dealing with his problems. He says, "I might be hit, but I'm not done. When the light comes, I'll start to rebuild." This change from blaming to just getting on with things, is a sign of Brian's new maturity.

In the following pages, you will learn how to write each of the parts of a body paragraph.

4.2 Body Paragraph – Topic Sentence

LEARN

The **topic sentence** is the first sentence in a body paragraph. The topic sentence states the main point that you will make in this paragraph. The main point will be one of the reasons listed in your thesis statement.

Use the outline you created previously to know what your topic sentence will be about. Here are several examples of topic sentences that support a thesis statement.

Thesis statement:

> In the novel *Hatchet*, the challenge of surviving alone forces Brian to mature from a child into a young man.

Good topic sentences:

- One sign of increasing maturity is that Brian stops blaming other people for things going wrong.

- Another sign of Brian's maturity is his increasing patience.

Both of these topic sentences directly support the claim Brian matures during the book. They each give one reason why the claim is true.

Poor topic sentence:

- Brian faces a lot of challenges in this book.

This is not a good topic sentence. It might be true, but it does not directly support the claim that Brian matures during the book.

4.2 Body Paragraph – Topic Sentence

PRACTICE

Use thesis statements that you have created previously and brainstorm 2-3 topic sentences for each.

Book/Movie + Thesis Statement	
Potential Topic Sentences	

Book/Movie + Thesis Statement	
Potential Topic Sentences	

4.2 Body Paragraph – Provide Evidence and Examples

LEARN

After the topic sentence, you provide **evidence (reasons you think it's true)** for the statement you made in your topic sentence. You then include an **example or quote** from the book that supports the evidence.

Use the following template to organize your paragraph.

TOPIC SENTENCE - EVIDENCE/EXPLANATION - SPECIFIC EXAMPLE or QUOTE

Here's an example.

Thesis statement:

In the novel *Hatchet*, the challenge of surviving alone forces Brian to mature from a child into a young man.

Topic Sentence:

One sign of increasing maturity is that Brian stops blaming other people for things going wrong.

Supporting Evidence/Explanation:

For example, in chapter 4, Brian thinks that if his mother hadn't forced the divorce, Brian wouldn't be stuck in the wilderness. Later on in chapter 15 after a terrible tornado, Brian doesn't worry about blaming anyone and instead just deals with his problems.

Quote:

He says, "I might be hit, but I'm not done. When the light comes, I'll start to rebuild." (p146)

4.2 Body Paragraph – Provide Evidence and Examples

LEARN

As you can see, this paragraph provides examples that support the topic sentence.

- The writer shows how Brian's first response was previously to blame other people.

- The writer then shows that later in the book Brian's response is to just deal with his problems.

- The paragraph also includes a quote that demonstrates Brian's new approach.

Important Note:

When you include an example or quote from the book, you must identify **where** the example came from.

- With a book, you can refer to a chapter number or page number.

- With a movie or play, you can refer to the scene with a short description.

  For example, if *Hatchet* was a movie:

  Brian's new attitude can be seen in the scene where he decides to rebuild after the tornado.

4.2 Body Paragraph – Provide Evidence and Examples

PRACTICE

Find a topic sentence that you have already written. Search the book to find examples that support your topic sentence. See if you can find a quote to match. Make sure to include a page or chapter number for each mention of events that happen in the book.

Topic Sentence:_____

Supporting Evidence/Explanation:	Relevant Quotes:

Topic Sentence:_____

Supporting Evidence/Explanation:	Relevant Quotes:

4.2 Body Paragraph – Link Back to Essay Claim

LEARN

The last step in writing your body paragraph is to connect your evidence back to the original claim.

To do this, you:

- Summarize the main point of the paragraph. (Say the same thing as your topic sentence but use different words.)

- State explicitly that the main point supports your claim. (Here ' state explicitly' means you put it into words. You don't assume the reader makes the link.)

Here's an example.

Thesis statement:

In the novel *Hatchet*, the challenge of surviving alone forces Brian to change from a child into a young man.

Body Paragraph Topic Sentence:

One sign of growing up is that Brian stops blaming other people for things going wrong.

Link Back: Good example:

This change from blaming to getting on with things, is a sign of Brian's new maturity.

This example has re-stated the topic sentence (Brian stops blaming people). The example also states that this information supports the claim (Brian becomes more mature.)

4.2 Body Paragraph – Link Back to Essay Claim

LEARN continued

Link Back: Bad example:

So, from these examples we can see that Brian stops blaming people.

This final sentence does summarize the main point (Brian stops blaming other people). But there is no link back the overall claim (Brian is becoming more mature.)

4.2 Body Paragraph – Link Back to Essay Claim

PRACTICE

Use examples from previous practices and write a sentence that links back to the original claim.

| **Thesis Statement:** |
| **Topic Sentence:** |
| **Supporting Evidence: (Notes or sentences)** |
| **Linking Sentence:** |

| **Thesis Statement:** |
| **Topic Sentence:** |
| **Supporting Evidence: (Notes or sentences)** |
| **Linking Sentence:** |

4.2 Complete Body Paragraph

PRACTICE

You are now ready to write a complete body paragraph. Write a body paragraph for a fiction or non-fiction book or video.

Use any of the examples you have created earlier.

Don't forget to include a topic sentence, examples and a quote, and the link back to the claim.

_____

_____

_____

_____

_____

_____

_____

4.3 Writing the Conclusion – Overview

LEARN

The concluding paragraph is the final paragraph in your essay. You have come a long way!

The final paragraph consists of:

- Restatement of thesis statement

- Final thoughts

The next lessons will teach you how to do these steps.

4.3 Writing the Conclusion - Restate Thesis

LEARN

In the conclusion, you remind your reader of the claims and evidence you provided in the book report.

You do this by restating your thesis statement. This means you say the same thing as your original thesis statement but use different words. Use more than one sentence if you need to.

Here's an example.

Original Thesis statement:

Through the challenges of finding food, building a shelter and trying to stay positive, Brian changes from a child into a young man.

Reworded Thesis Statement:

In *Hatchet*, being alone in the wild makes Brian change. His need for food, shelter and trying to stay positive, means he must act more like an adult than a kid.

Another (More Advanced) Example:

In conclusion, in *Hatchet*, the adversity of surviving alone forces Brian to mature from a child into a young man. His need for sufficient food, reliable shelter and maintaining his will to survive, requires Brian to leave behind the comfort of childhood and take on the responsibilities that maturity brings.

4.3 Writing the Conclusion - Reword Thesis

PRACTICE

Practice restating thesis statements. For the last two lines, use thesis statements that you have written in previous practice pages.

Original Thesis Statement	Reworded Thesis Statement
Brian's biggest strength is his determination. His determination led to lighting fire, catching food, and recovering the all-important hatchet.	

4.3 Writing the Conclusion - Final Thoughts

LEARN

Conclude your book report by adding a final thought. The final thought sentence brings your report to a close.

There are several ways to add a final thought to your book report.

- Add a Future Thought

- Add an Encouragement to Action

- Add a Question about the Content

- Add a Personal Opinion

Here are some examples of how each of these strategies could be used in a final paragraph. Depending on the book, some final thoughts work better than others.

Using the usual *Hatchet* example.

A question about the content:

> How do you think you would fare if you had to survive in the wilderness?

A personal opinion/future thought:

> I hope that if I ever faced Brian's challenges, I would develop the same maturity.

Using the non-fiction book *A Child Through Time* example:

An encouragement to action:

> DK Publishing has produced a fascinating and educational book. Let's hope DK produces more of these interesting books.

4.3 Adding Final Thoughts

PRACTICE

Write several final thought sentences for each example. Use thesis statements that you have developed in previous practices.

Thesis Statement:
Final Thoughts:

Thesis Statement:
Final Thoughts:

4.3 Complete Final Paragraph

PRACTICE

You are now ready to write a complete final paragraph. Write a final paragraph for a fiction or non-fiction book or video.

You can use examples from previous practice pages.

Don't forget to include the reworded thesis statement and a final thought.

_____

_____

_____

_____

_____

_____

_____

Putting It All Together
Writing a Complete
Book Report

You have learned a lot about how to complete a book report. Now let's put your skills to work in creating some wonderful writing.

On the next page is a handy checklist for each stage of the process. Use this checklist any time you have a book report assignment.

You can download a PDF of this checklist for easy printing from:

http://www.HappyFrogLearning.com/product/book-report-checklist

Book Report Checklist

Before You Read

- ❑ Analyze the assignment instructions
- ❑ Review unknown words
- ❑ Choose your book
- ❑ Understand the genre expectations
- ❑ Prepare the reading questions

While You Read

- ❑ Plan your reading schedule
- ❑ Read & take notes

After You Read

- ❑ Review notes and create thesis statement
- ❑ Convert thesis statement into outline

Write the Report

- ❑ Write the introductory paragraph
- ❑ Write the body paragraphs
- ❑ Write the conclusion

Part 2

Reference Section

Part 2 contains:

- A **FAQ** where you can find answers to common questions that students have about book reports.

- **Explanations** for a variety of common **literary devices**.

FAQ

In this section we provide answers to questions you may have about your particular assignment.

You will find that the common answer is… **follow the guidelines introduced in this book** and you will have no trouble.

However, some book assignments do have slight differences. Review these answers to reassure yourself that you are on the right track.

I Need to Write a Book Review. How is That Different?

To write a **book review**, follow the process outlined in this book. One difference is that the claim can be your opinion on whether the book is good or not.

Here is an example of a claim for a review:

- *Hatchet* is an exciting book that should be read by all middle school students.

Here are two example thesis statements that would work for a review:

- Because of its wonderful drawings and interesting information, *A Child Through Time* should be included in every school library.

- Despite its popularity, *book name* is badly written, contains boring characters and is very predictable. No kid should have to read this.

As you can see, each gives an opinion about whether other people should read the book. As usual, the claim is supported by reasons.

My Teacher Says She Wants a Literary Analysis. What is That?

A **literary analysis or literary essay** is an essay where your claim is about how a literary device is used in the book. Don't know what literary devices are? Don't worry, they are explained later in this workbook.

Some examples of literary devices are 'character' and 'plot'. A claim about 'character' could be something like: The main character becomes stronger through the book.

So, learn abut the literary device that you have been assigned. Then, follow the instructions you learned in this book: Develop a thesis statement and provide reasons/evidence from the book to support your claim.

I Need to Analyze a Poem. How is That Different?

Analyzing a poem might seem like a challenge, but the process is the same as analyzing a book. Follow the instructions in this book and you will end up with an excellent report.

One difference with poem analysis is the topics you write about. There are many literary devices that are common in poetry. These include figurative language, imagery, metaphors, similes, personification, assonance, and alliteration... to name just a few.

You will find that poem assignments tend to ask about these types of topics. This is different from fiction book assignments which tend to be about character or conflict.

But don't worry, follow the process described in this book and you will create an excellent assignment. Just make sure you understand the literary device you must write about.

My Teacher Says She Wants a Simple Book Report. What is That?

If your teacher is asking for **a simple book report**, she may be looking for a report that includes some or all of the following paragraphs.

1. Introduction
2. Book Details: Setting
3. Book Details: Characters
4. Book Details: Plot
5. Evaluation and Conclusion

It's best to ask your teacher directly so you know for sure.

Make sure to follow the guidelines in this book and craft a thesis statement. Even a 'simple' book report is easier to write if you have a clear thesis statement.

Your thesis statement could be something as straightforward as:

> With diverse characters, a surprising plot and an unusual setting, *book-name* by *book-author* provides an exciting read for lovers of mysteries.

This thesis statement helps you decide what to write in each paragraph: Your character paragraph will discuss the diversity of the characters, your plot paragraph will explain how it is surprising, and your setting paragraph will explain how it is unusual.

I Need to Write About a Movie or a Live Play. How is That Different?

For the most part, writing about **a movie or play** is the same as writing about a book. Just follow the process described in this workbook. However, there are a few extra things to think about.

1. For a play: read the play before you attend the performance. You should make notes as you read the play, just like you would when reading a book. However, as you read, also add new questions about what you want to consider while you are watching the play.

2. At the play or movie, consider these issues: Setting, lighting, music, costumes, acting, direction - anything about the performance.

Afterwards, create your thesis statement as usual to meet the requirements of your assignment. However, as evidence, you can refer to the performance as well as the story.

My Book is Non-Fiction. How is That Different?

If your report is for a **non-fiction book**, follow the same process outlined in this book. As usual, you will need a thesis statement and supporting arguments.

However, the topics you write about will be a little different. Plot, character and conflict are common when writing about fiction. But with non-fiction, you will consider topics such as the following:

1. What is the author's goal with the book?

2. How well did the author meet this goal?

3. What are the author's qualifications?

4. What is the central idea discussed in the book?

5. What evidence does the author use to support the book's ideas?

6. What kind of language does the author use?

7. What have you learned after reading this book?

Apart from the different topics, the rest of the book report process is the same. Follow the steps in this book to arrive at your thesis statement, and then write the report.

Here are some examples of thesis statements and claims for non-fiction books.

- Because of its beautiful illustrations and interesting information, *A Child Through Time* should be included in every school library.

- *Author-name's* book about gardens, while intended for teens, is too simple for this audience.

- *Author-name's* biography of *name* is a heartwarming, educational and surprising look at this famous actor's life.

Are There Any Formatting Tips I should Know?

Watch out for these difference from other writing you might do.

1. Make sure you **include the chapter or page number** for all examples you mention. You can include the page number in the text of your sentence, or at the end of the sentence in brackets.

   - An example of Brian's determination is when he tries to make a fire for hours and hours (p 82).

   - An example of Brian's determination is found in chapter 9 when he tried to make a fire.

2. If you **quote directly** from the text, **put the quote in quotation marks.** Also make sure you quote word for word from the text.

   - "I will have a fire here, he thought, and struck again—I will have fire from the hatchet." (p81)

3. If you do **an indirect quote, do not use quotation marks. Also,** do not quote word for word. You should put the content in your own words.

   - A similar example can be found when Brian decides that he will make a fire, (p81).

4. The name of the book should be in italics or single quotation marks. Choose one method and use it throughout your report.

   - In the novel *Hatchet*, Gary Paulsen tells an amazing story.

   - In the novel 'Hatchet', Gary Paulsen tells an amazing story.

Common Literary Devices

This section introduces 25 common **literary devices.** Usually, a book report assignment asks about one or two literary devices. To write one report, you don't need to be an expert on all of them.

These descriptions are intended to be **a review or reminder** of each literary device. If these terms are completely new to you, you may want to find a more in-depth source of information.

Literary devices fall into two main categories: literary elements and literary techniques. (See the diagram on the next page.)

Literary elements are parts of a story that are not dependent on the words chosen by the author. Examples of literary elements are plot, characters, and point of view.

Literary techniques are parts of a text that result from an author choosing specific words and phrases. Examples of literary techniques are foreshadowing, allegories, and figurative language. **Figurative language** includes a variety of different strategies such as idioms, metaphors, and allusion.

In the following pages, the literary devices are listed alphabetically.

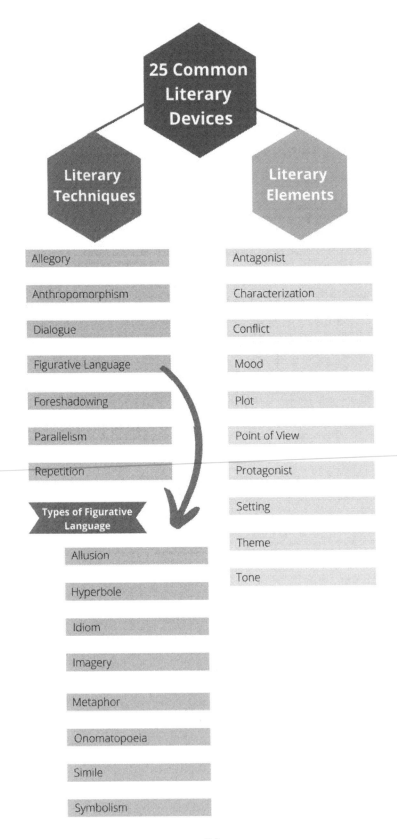

25 Common Literary Devices

Literary Techniques

- Allegory
- Anthropomorphism
- Dialogue
- Figurative Language
- Foreshadowing
- Parallelism
- Repetition

Types of Figurative Language

- Allusion
- Hyperbole
- Idiom
- Imagery
- Metaphor
- Onomatopoeia
- Simile
- Symbolism

Literary Elements

- Antagonist
- Characterization
- Conflict
- Mood
- Plot
- Point of View
- Protagonist
- Setting
- Theme
- Tone

Allegory

An allegory is a story that contains an extra meaning beyond the original story.

For example, in *The Lorax*, the hidden meaning is that we should look after our environment. The story describes what could happen in our world.

Antagonist

The antagonist is the main person or force who works against the main character, or who prevents the main character from reaching her goals.

For example, Darth Vader is the antagonist in *Star Wars*. Voldemort is the antagonist in *Harry Potter*.

Allusion

An allusion is a reference to something that the writer assumes the reader knows about. It can be a person, place, thing, event, piece of art or popular culture. The writer wants the reader to get extra meaning by knowing about the alluded event/item.

For example, in the following sentence, the writer assumes the reader knows about Superman. Kryptonite is the one thing that makes superman weak.

Ice-cream is my kryptonite.

In the next example, the writer assumes the reader knows about Scrooge (from a well-known story). Scrooge is very careful with money.

You are such a scrooge.

Anthropomorphism

Anthropomorphism is the when the writer gives human feelings or intentions to non-human things like animals and plants.

For example, in the story *The Three Little Pigs*, the pigs and the wolf talk and act like humans. Another example of anthropomorphism is Mickey Mouse, who also acts and talks like a human.

Characterization

Characterization happens any time the author tells us about a character in the story.

Direct characterization is when the author explicitly tells us what a character is like.

For example, Harry Potter is directly described as follows: "Harry had a thin face, knobbly knees, black hair, and bright green eyes." We are told exactly what Harry looks like.

Indirect characterization occurs when the reader has to guess information from what is written.

For example, in *Harry Potter*, the house elf Dobby refers to Harry as "the noble Harry Potter." From this we can guess (or infer) that Dobby likes Harry. We are not told this directly, but we can infer it and add it to our information about Dobby.

Conflict

Conflict: The challenges that the main character faces that force him/her to take action in the story.

All conflict can be classified as either internal conflict or external conflict.

Internal conflict is when a character struggles with their own wants and thoughts. This type of conflict is called 'character versus self'.

External conflict is when a character has to fight or work against something or someone external to themselves. There are several types of external conflict.

- Character versus Character

    - An example is Harry Potter versus Voldemort in the *Harry Potter* series.

- Character versus Nature

    - An example is Brian Robeson's fight to survive in *Hatchet*.

- Character versus Supernatural

    - An example is Harry Potter versus Voldemort in the *Harry Potter* series as Voldemort has supernatural powers.

- Character versus Technology

    - An example is the story of *Frankenstein.* Dr Frankenstein creates a monster who then tries to kill him.

- Character versus Society

    - An example is *Hunger Games* where the main character attempts to change how society is run.

Dialogue

Dialogue refers to the words spoken by characters in a story. It is usually an interaction between two or more characters, though it is possible to have a character talking to themselves occasionally.

Dialogue plays a large part in almost all works of fiction. Plays and movies are almost entirely dialogue.

In written work, dialogue is shown by specific punctuation. For example:

John said, "That is crazy."

Figurative Language

Figurative language refers to words and phrases that have an additional meaning instead of (or in addition to) the actual meaning of the words.

Idioms are an example of figurative language. The idiom 'kick the bucket' means that someone died. The literal meaning of someone kicking an actual bucket is not part of the meaning.

There are many types of figurative language, such as metaphor, simile, hyperbole and allusion. You can find explanations for many of these in this section.

Foreshadowing

Foreshadowing is when the author gives hints about what will happen later in the story. These clues can increase the tension/mood.

An example of foreshadowing in *Harry Potter* is Harry's visit to the zoo in the first book. In that scene, Harry releases a snake from its cage. When the snake thanks him, Harry understands what he says. This is the first clue that Harry speaks the snake language Parseltongue.

Foreshadowing can be done through a character's action or words. It can also be done through other aspects, like the setting. For example, stormy weather often foreshadows serious events in horror or mystery novels.

Hyperbole

Hyperbole is when you exaggerate when describing something. Using hyperbole makes your description more dramatic. Readers understand it is hyperbole because the description is not realistic.

An example of hyperbole:

> Kerry sighed, "I ate a million chips today."

Kerry is not trying to say that she actually ate a million chips today. She is exaggerating to make her point that a LOT of chips were eaten.

Idiom

An idiom is a common expression that has a different meaning than the literal meaning of the words. Idioms are a type of figurative language.

For example, to say that someone 'kicked the bucket' means that they died, not that they actually kicked a bucket.

Imagery

Imagery is when an author helps the reader imagine the smell, taste, touch, sight, and sound in a story.

For example, the following example uses the word 'velvet-soft' to help us imagine how soft the kitten's fur is.

> Kayla stroked the kitten's velvet-soft fur.

In the following example, the word 'blanket' helps us see how thick the leaves are on the ground.

> The autumn leaves blanketed the ground.

Metaphor

A metaphor compares two objects in a way that isn't literally true, but which shows something they have in common. It is phrased as *something **is** something*.

For example, the metaphor 'My love is an ocean,' is not literally true. The author wants the reader to understand that the love is big or vast like an ocean.

Metaphor is a type of figurative language. The reader has to figure out what the intended comparison is.

Mood

Mood is the overall feeling or atmosphere of a piece of writing. It is the feeling the reader has as they read the text.

There are many words that can describe the mood of a text: scary, sad, humorous, hopeful, depressing, etc.

The events of the story and how they are described help us feel the mood. Compare the following two examples, which show a happy/excited mood versus a low key/low energy mood.

> The dog spied the overflowing food dish and tugged on his leash. He gave a happy yip as he lunged toward the food.

> The dog slouched on the floor and ignored the overflowing food dish.

Onomatopoeia

Onomatopoeia is when a word actually sounds like the object (or action) it refers to. Writers use onomatopoeia to bring a story or poem to life in the reader's head.

Examples of onomatopoeia include the words 'grumble,' 'yawn,' and 'hush.'

Parallelism

Parallelism is when an author uses phrasing that is similar or identical in structure, sound, meaning, or rhythm. The similar words/phrases need to appear close to each other.

An example of parallelism is Neil Armstrong's statement, made as he stepped on the moon:

> "That's one small step for man, one giant leap for mankind."

The 'one small step' and 'one giant leap' have parallel structure. Armstrong made his statement more memorable by using parallel structure.

Plot

The plot is the sequence of events that makes up the story. A plot usually has the following five stages.

1. **Exposition**: This is where the characters and setting are introduced at the beginning of the book. The main character encounters a problem that drives his/her actions through the rest of the book.

2. **Rising Action**: This includes all the actions and events where the main character is trying to solve his/her problem. Usually the stakes get higher as the book progresses. This section forms the majority of the book.

3. **Climax**: This point is usually the most exciting. The main character faces his/her biggest challenge and the outcome leads to the end of the book.

4. **Falling Action**: The follow-up to the climax. Loose ends start to get tied up. Sub-plots get tidied up.

5. **Resolution**: The final outcome is described.

Point of View

Point of view (POV) refers to the type of narrator a writer chooses to tell the story.

There are five different points of view.

First Person POV

First person POV is told from the point of view of the writer themselves. You can recognize first person POV by the narrator of the story using the pronouns 'I' and 'We'.

I agreed to go to the game, even though I didn't want to.

Second Person POV

Second person POV is recognized by the use of 'You' by the narrator. With the second person POV the narrator is telling you **your** story. It is unusual to find second person POV.

You agreed to go to the game, even though you didn't want to.

Third Person POV

There are three types of third person points of view.

Third Person Objective

With 3rd person objective POV, the story is told in third person, but we do not get to see 'inside' anyone's head. So the only way we can know about any character's thoughts and feelings is by what they say or do.

With a smile, Jo agreed to go to the game. Jack grinned back at her.

Here we can see the action, but we don't know anyone's thoughts and feelings beyond what they say and do.

Point of View continued

Third Person Limited

With 3rd person limited POV, the story is told in third person, and we get to see inside one character's head for the duration of a scene or section. We can learn directly about that character's thoughts and feelings, but other characters' thoughts and feelings can only be inferred by what they say or do.

With a smile, Jo agreed to go to the game, even though she didn't really want to. Jack grinned back at her, so she knew she'd done the right thing.

Here we see Jo's thoughts, but not Jack's.

Third Person Omniscient

With 3rd person omniscient POV, the story is told in third person, and we get to see inside many characters' heads. We learn directly about many characters' thoughts and feelings.

With a smile, Jo agreed to go to the game, even though she didn't really want to. Jack grinned at Jo, hoping his disappointment didn't show.

Here we see Jo's thoughts and Jack's thoughts.

Protagonist

The protagonist is the main character in a story. It is this character that has the biggest problem in the book and it is their actions which drive the story.

In the *Harry Potter* books, Harry is the protagonist. In the novel *Hatchet*, Brian is the protagonist.

Repetition

Repetition is when the writer uses the same word or phrase over and over again throughout the book.

Note:

Repetition is the reuse of words, phrases, ideas or themes throughout a book. **Parallelism** has two or more phrases with identical or similar structure appearing close to each other.

Setting

The setting is where and when a story or event takes place. Authors can describe a setting to include location, time, weather, and environment. The setting can influence the actions or events of a story.

For example, a murder mystery is scarier if the setting is an island where escape is impossible.

Simile

A simile compares two things, usually in a phrase with 'as' or 'like.' A simile is a type of figurative language. This means its meaning is more than the literal meaning of the words.

For example: 'the girl's hands were as cold as ice'.

The author uses a comparison with ice to show that the girl's hands were very cold. The writer does not literally mean that her hands were the same temperature as ice.

Note: Similes are often confused with metaphors. Similes use 'like' or 'as.' Metaphors say something 'is' something else.

Symbolism

Symbolism is when a writer uses something to mean more than its original meaning.

For example, if a character often wears red , this may be a symbol that represents the character's fiery nature.

Words, people, marks, locations or ideas can all be symbols.

Theme

Theme is the underlying message that you can take away from a story. The theme is never directly stated. It is figured out by determining what 'lesson' can be learned from the story.

To determine the theme, look at what the characters learned (or should have learned) through the story.

A book can have more than one theme. For example, one theme in *Harry Potter* is the importance of confronting fears. Another is the importance of accepting death. Yet another theme is the acceptance of others with differing backgrounds and beliefs.

Tone

Tone is the attitude the author has towards the reader or the subject of a text. The tone is shown by the author's word choices.

Tone can be described using words such as sympathetic, cheerful, outraged, positive, angry, sarcastic, ironic, intense, excited, humorous, etc.

You can see differences in tone in the following examples. The first is grimmer and the second has an element of humour and lightness.

- The ball sailed through the air and smashed through the window, leaving a dark jagged gash. John's stomach clenched. "Mom is going to kill me."

- The ball sailed through the air and smashed through the window. The glass shattered like a shower of confetti. John grimaced. "Well, that didn't go as planned."

Conclusion

Congratulations on finishing the workbook!

You now know everything you need to know to write a book report, book review, or literary essay. Well done!

Why don't you check out the other books in the Step-by-Step Study Skills series?

We especially recommend the *How to Edit and Revise Your Essay* workbook as the editing skills will make your book report even stronger.

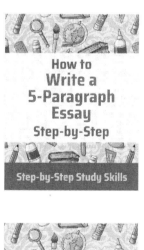

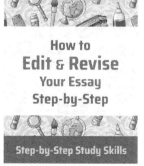

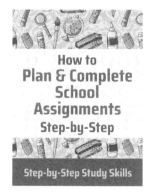

CERTIFICATE
OF
ACHIEVEMENT

THIS CERTIFICATE IS AWARDED TO

_____

IN RECOGNITION OF

_____

_____   _____

DATE   **SIGNATURE**

_____

TITLE

Printed in Great Britain
by Amazon

36061646R00051